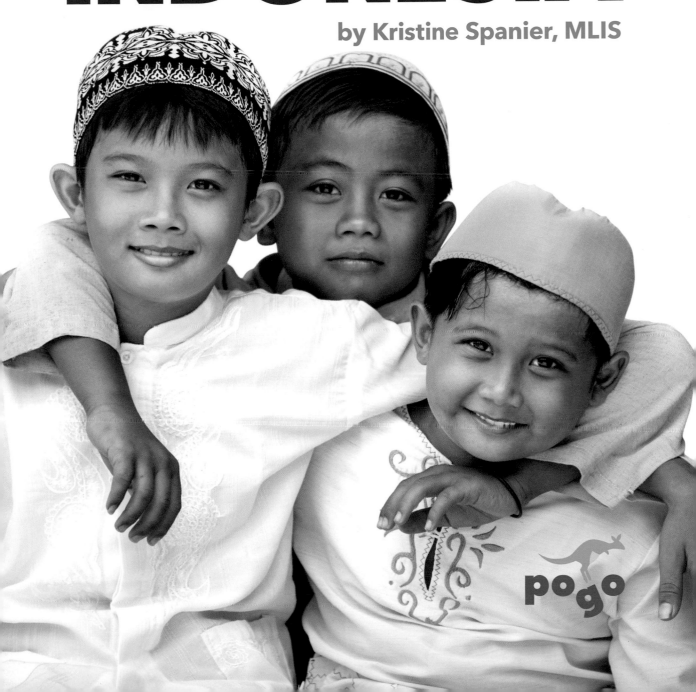

ALL AROUND THE WORLD
INDONESIA

by Kristine Spanier, MLIS

pogo

Ideas for Parents and Teachers

Pogo Books let children practice reading informational text while introducing them to nonfiction features such as headings, labels, sidebars, maps, and diagrams, as well as a table of contents, glossary, and index.

Carefully leveled text with a strong photo match offers early fluent readers the support they need to succeed.

Before Reading

- "Walk" through the book and point out the various nonfiction features. Ask the student what purpose each feature serves.
- Look at the glossary together. Read and discuss the words.

Read the Book

- Have the child read the book independently.
- Invite him or her to list questions that arise from reading.

After Reading

- Discuss the child's questions. Talk about how he or she might find answers to those questions.
- Prompt the child to think more. Ask: Indonesia includes many different islands. How is this similar to or different from where you live?

Pogo Books are published by Jump!
5357 Penn Avenue South
Minneapolis, MN 55419
www.jumplibrary.com

Library of Congress Cataloging-in-Publication Data

Names: Spanier, Kristine, author.
Title: Indonesia / by Kristine Spanier.
Description: Minneapolis, MN: Pogo Books, 2021.
Series: All around the world | Includes index.
Audience: Ages 7-10 | Audience: Grades 2-3
Identifiers: LCCN 2019041563 (print)
LCCN 2019041564 (ebook)
ISBN 9781645273387 (hardcover)
ISBN 9781645273394 (paperback)
ISBN 9781645273400 (ebook)
Subjects: LCSH: Indonesia–Juvenile literature.
Classification: LCC DS615 .S63 2021 (print)
LCC DS615 (ebook) | DDC 959.8–dc23
LC record available at https://lccn.loc.gov/2019041563
LC ebook record available at https://lccn.loc.gov/2019041564

Editor: Jenna Gleisner
Designer: Molly Ballanger

Photo Credits: Khoroshunova Olga/Shutterstock, cover; Distinctive Images/Shutterstock, 1; Pixfiction/Shutterstock, 3; Aum-ng/iStock, 4; Elena Odareeva/Shutterstock, 5; sergemi/Shutterstock, 6-7; Eric Isselee/Shutterstock, 8; Yavuz Sariyildiz/Shutterstock, 9; David Yeo/Getty, 10-11tl; iStock, 10-11tr; Cyril Ruoso/Minden Pictures/SuperStock, 10-11bl; Dennis van de Water/Shutterstock, 10-11br; Amnat Phuthamrong/Shutterstock, 12-13; Reca Ence AR/Shutterstock, 14tl; szefei/Shutterstock, 14tr; bonchan/Shutterstock, 14b; Adifruslan/Shutterstock, 15; Manamana/Shutterstock, 16-17; INDONESIAPIX/Shutterstock, 18-19; aditya_frzhm/Shutterstock, 20-21; Melimey/Shutterstock, 23.

Printed in the United States of America at Corporate Graphics in North Mankato, Minnesota.

TABLE OF CONTENTS

CHAPTER 1

WELCOME TO INDONESIA!

Mount Merapi

What country has 130 **active volcanoes**? Indonesia! Mount Merapi is the most active.

Volcanic rock breaks down to make black sand. This makes black sand beaches! Welcome!

Indonesia is an **archipelago**. It has more than 17,500 islands! This means there are many beaches. There is even a pink sand beach here! A **coral reef** is nearby. The pink color comes from creatures that once lived in the reef.

DID YOU KNOW?

The **equator** passes through Indonesia. The **climate** is hot and humid. But **glaciers** are in the mountains!

coral reef

CHAPTER 2

ONE COUNTRY, MANY ISLANDS

People live on more than 7,000 of the islands. Do you want to visit Komodo? This island has giant lizards! Komodo dragons grow up to 10 feet (3 meters) long!

Komodo dragon

Bali's biggest **crop** is rice. It grows on **terraces** here. Most of this island is covered with mountains. The highest point is Mount Agung. It is 9,888 feet (3,014 m) high.

rice terrace

Flying lemurs and gibbons live in the trees of Sumatra. So do orangutans. The two-horned Sumatran rhino is here, too. Tea and coffee crops are grown here for **exports**.

flying lemur

gibbon

Sumatran rhino

orangutan

Jakarta

About half of the **population** lives on Java. The **capital** is on this island. It is Jakarta. This city is very crowded. People get around on buses, trains, taxis, and bikes.

WHAT DO YOU THINK?

More than 700 languages are spoken here! Indonesia's **motto** is "**unity** in **diversity**." What does this mean to you? How can diverse people find unity?

Hello!

Halo!

CHAPTER 3

LIFE IN INDONESIA

Food is full of flavor here! Satay is a skewer of chicken or vegetables. Rendang is spicy meat. Martabak is sweet fried bread. Rice is served at almost every meal.

martabak

satay

beef rendang

Fabric artists use wax and dye. They make patterns on cloth. This is called batik. It is turned into bright clothing.

batik

Buddhist and Hindu **temples** are here. The Borobudur Temple was built between 778 and 850 CE. It was created to honor Buddha.

Borobudur Temple

Buddha

TAKE A LOOK!

In the 1300s, Muslim **traders** came here. They brought their religion with them. Indonesia is now home to the world's largest Muslim population. What other religions do people follow here?

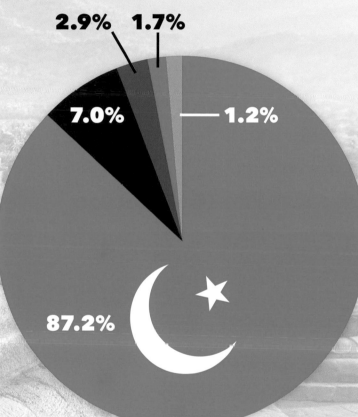

2.9% 1.7%

7.0%

1.2%

87.2%

- ■ = Muslim
- ■ = Protestant
- ■ = Roman Catholic
- ■ = Hindu
- ■ = other or unspecified

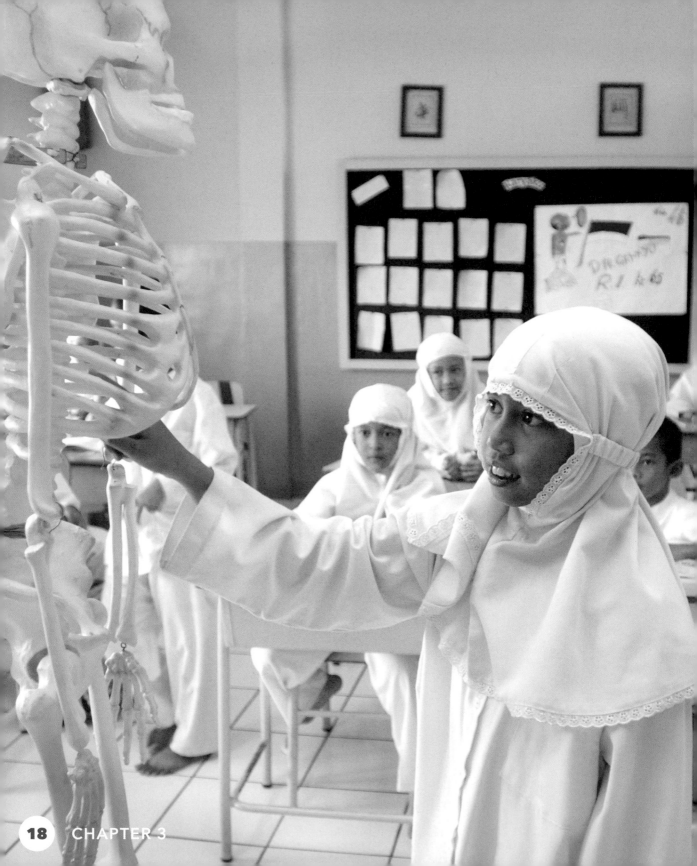

Most children here start school when they are seven years old. They must go for at least nine years. They study many subjects, including math, science, and religion.

Children in **rural** areas might not finish school. Why? They need to help with chores. Children in cities usually go to school longer.

Badminton and soccer are popular. So is sepak takraw. It is like volleyball. But it is played with feet! Flying kites is another favorite activity. There are even kite festivals!

There are many fun things to do in this country. Would you like to visit?

WHAT DO YOU THINK?

Public storytelling is popular here. It is a way to remember the past. Does your family share stories from the past? Are they about people or events?

QUICK FACTS & TOOLS

INDONESIA

Location: Southeast Asia

Size: 735,358 square miles
(1,904,569 square kilometers)

Population: 262,787,403
(July 2018 estimate)

Capital: Jakarta

Type of Government:
presidential republic

Languages: Bahasa Indonesia,
English, Dutch, Javanese

Exports: rubber, mineral fuels,
animal and vegetable fats,
electrical machinery

Currency: Indonesian rupiah

GLOSSARY

active: An active volcano is one that has had at least one eruption during the past 10,000 years.

archipelago: A group of islands.

capital: A city where government leaders meet.

climate: The weather typical of a certain place over a long period of time.

coral reef: A strip of coral close to the surface of the ocean or another body of water.

crop: A plant grown for food.

diversity: A variety.

equator: An imaginary line around the center of Earth.

exports: Products sold to different countries.

glaciers: Very large, slow-moving masses of ice.

motto: A short phrase that states a belief.

population: The total number of people who live in a place.

rural: Related to the country and country life.

temples: Buildings used for worship.

terraces: Raised, flat platforms of land with sloping sides.

traders: People who buy and sell goods.

unity: The state of being united or joined as a whole.

volcanoes: Mountains with openings through which molten lava, ash, and hot gases erupt.

Indonesia's currency

INDEX

TO LEARN MORE

Finding more information is as easy as 1, 2, 3.

❶ Go to www.factsurfer.com

❷ Enter "Indonesia" into the search box.

❸ Click the "Surf" button to see a list of websites.

FACT SURFER